DOUBLEDAY THEATER SERIES

BAKER STREET

BAKER STREET

A Musical Adventure of Sherlock Holmes

Book by
JEROME COOPERSMITH

Music and Lyrics by
MARIAN GRUDEFF *and* RAYMOND JESSEL

Adapted from the Stories by
SIR ARTHUR CONAN DOYLE

DOUBLEDAY & COMPANY, INC. GARDEN CITY, NEW YORK 1966

Photographs by courtesy of Friedman-Abeles

Lyrics by Marian Grudeff and Raymond Jessel used by permission of Edward B. Marks Music Corporation.

Library of Congress Catalog Card Number 66–12179

Printed in the United States of America
First Edition

BAKER STREET was first presented by Alexander H. Cohen at the Broadway Theatre, New York City, on February 16, 1965, with the following cast:

(In order of appearance)

SHERLOCK HOLMES	Fritz Weaver
CAPTAIN GREGG	Patrick Horgan
DR. WATSON	Peter Sallis
MRS. HUDSON	Paddy Edwards
INSPECTOR LESTRADE	Daniel Keyes
IRENE ADLER	Inga Swenson
DAISY	Virginia Vestoff
BAXTER	Martin Wolfson
WIGGINS	Teddy Green
DUCKBELLOWS	Bert Michaels
NIPPER	Sal Pernice
PERKINS	George Lee
MACIPPER	Mark Jude Sheil
MURILLO	Jay Norman
THE THREE KILLERS	Avin Harum, Christopher Walken, Tommy Tune
TAVERN SINGER	Gwenn Lewis
PROFESSOR MORIARTY	Martin Gabel

Book by Jerome Coopersmith
Music and Lyrics by Marian Grudeff and Raymond Jessel
Choreography by Lee Becker Theodore
Production Directed by Harold Prince
Production Designed by Oliver Smith
Lighting by Jean Rosenthal
Costumes Designed by Motley
Musical Direction by Harold Hastings
Orchestrations by Don Walker
Dance Arrangements by John Morris
Orchestra Conducted by Arthur Wagner
Diamond Jubilee Parade by Bil Baird's Marionettes

SCENE SYNOPSIS

Act I

Prologue: Baker Street, London. A night in 1897.
Scene 1: The Baker Street flat. Time, the same.
Scene 2: The stage of the Theatre Royal. Later that night.
Scene 3: Backstage at the Theatre Royal. Time, the same.
Scene 4: An alley in Baker Street. Early the next morning.
Scene 5: Irene's house. The same morning.
Scene 6: Outside the Buckingham Palace Gate. A few hours later.
Scene 7: The Baker Street flat. Later that day.
Scene 8: The London underworld. All through the night.
Scene 9: Moriarty's yacht. Early the next morning.

Act II

Scene 1: A street in London. Later that morning.
Scene 2: Moriarty's yacht. Time, several minutes later.
Scene 3: Interior of a four-wheeled carriage. That night.
Scene 4: The cliffs of Dover. Later that night.
Scene 5: A part of London. A few days later.
Scene 6: The Baker Street flat. Later that day.
Scene 7: A private funeral parlor. That night.

MUSICAL SYNOPSIS

Act I

1. "It's Simple"	HOLMES, WATSON, GREGG, LESTRADE
2. "Buffalo Belle"	IRENE and GIRLS
3. "Leave It to Us, Guv"	WIGGINS and THE IRREGULARS
4. "Letters"	IRENE
5. "The Cold, Clear World of the Intellect"	HOLMES
6. "Finding Words for Spring"	IRENE
7. "What a Night This Is Going to Be"	HOLMES, IRENE, WATSON, DAISY
9. "Underworld" Ballet	COMPANY
10. "I Shall Miss You"	MORIARTY

Act II

11. "Roof Space"	WIGGINS and THE IRREGULARS
12. "Married Man"	WATSON
13. "I'd Do It Again"	IRENE
14. "The Pursuit"	HOLMES
15. "Jewellery"	BAXTER and CRIMINALS

ACT I

Prologue

TIME: *A night in 1897.*

SCENE: *Baker Street, London.*

A street of austere brick and gray stone houses, each with an iron railing in front. The house at extreme right has a large bow window overlooking the street, but is otherwise indistinguishable from its neighbors.

The street is dark and forbidding. A heavy fog refracts all light into ill-defined yellow haze. Big Ben tolls ten, and somewhere in the distance we hear the clatter of hoofs and carriage wheels on a cobblestone road. As the clock-tower bell fades into silence, we become aware of another sound; a thin, plaintive melody being played on a hurdy-gurdy. The fog begins to lift, and we discern a stooped, elderly BEGGAR *playing this music in the arc of a gaslit street lamp. Nearby a* DRUNK *lies sprawled in a doorway.*

GREGG, *a handsome young man, enters from left. He refers to a piece of paper in his hand as he tries to read the numbers on the darkened buildings. He approaches the* DRUNK.

GREGG

Do you know what — (*The* DRUNK *mumbles something incoherent and flops over.* GREGG *turns to the* BEGGAR.) Do you know what number this is? I'm looking for 221B Baker Street. (*The* BEGGAR *barely shrugs.*) Well perhaps you know the man I'm looking for. Mr. Sherlock Holmes, a consulting detective. (*drops a coin in the* BEGGAR'S *cup*) Tall fellow, I'm told — sharp features — shares a flat with a medical chap — Dr. Watkins or something of the sort. (*A pause.* GREGG *drops another coin into the cup. Still no response from the* BEGGAR.) Now look, I've been walking up and down for the past twenty minutes looking for the blasted place— (*As* GREGG *talks, the lights come up behind the drawn shades of the large bow window facing the street. There we see the unmistakable silhouette of Sherlock Holmes.*) —Half the houses don't have any numbers on them, and those that do are so grimy, you can't tell a 221 from— (*noticing the silhouette in the window, he turns to the* BEGGAR) Thank you very much.

(GREGG *starts to enter* 221B. *Suddenly the* DRUNK *in the doorway—now sober—leaps to his feet, takes out a pistol, and fires two shots at the silhouette of Holmes. There is the sound of shattering glass, and the silhouette slumps forward.* GREGG *turns in the doorway and rushes toward the* DRUNK, *but is pushed to the ground. The* DRUNK *starts to flee, but finds his way blocked by the elderly* BEGGAR *who flings him to the ground and disarms him in one swift motion. As the* DRUNK *goes sprawling, the* BEGGAR *rips off a disguise to reveal himself as* SHERLOCK HOLMES. *He holds the* DRUNK *at bay with a pistol.*)

HOLMES

Good shooting, old man. Wrong target, I'm afraid. (*Takes a police whistle out of his pocket and blows a shrill blast. There is an echo of answering whistles offstage. The would-be assassin and* GREGG *watch* HOLMES *in shocked amazement.*)

Show curtain falls

(*Overture*)

ACT I

SCENE 1

TIME: *The same.*

SCENE: *The sitting room of the Baker Street flat, rented jointly by* SHERLOCK HOLMES *and* DR. JOHN WATSON.

It is a large, cluttered room with a door to the hallway up right, a door to Holmes's bedroom at the left, and a door to Watson's bedroom at the right. The room is a gaslit melange of Victorian trappings and bizarre mementos of crime. It contains a chemistry table overflowing with test tubes, siphons, and oddly shaped bottles; a bookcase bulging with ancient, ponderous reference volumes; and a chart of a human brain. Up center there is a fireplace complete with all the brass fittings of the 1890s. On the wall above the mantel, the initials "V.R." are spelled out boldly in bullet holes. Holmes's makeup table, cluttered with props for his many disguises, stands at extreme down right.

DR. WATSON *kneels near the window examining the waxen dummy, oblivious to* MRS. HUDSON *who stands over his shoulder. As she speaks,* WATSON *encircles a bullet hole with chalk.*

MRS. HUDSON

Oh, look what a lovely gift my gentlemen lodgers have given me now! Two days before the Diamond Jubilee, and me after scrubbing and polishing every last inch of the place to show proper respect for the queen. I thank them kindly for it.

WATSON

The window will be repaired, Mrs. Hudson.

MRS. HUDSON

The window will be repaired, he says——as if I would let them change one bit of this lovely elegance— (*saluting the* V. R. *bullet holes in the wall*) — Why those bullet holes in the wall never fail to stir up love of country— (*examines a knife which is pinning several bills and letters to the mantel*) — And put an end to this delicate filing system— (*pulls out the knife*) — Not in a million years— (*goes to the chemistry table*) — And how could I live without those sweet-smelling chemical acids seeping into my halls and floors.

(HOLMES *bursts in with* GREGG.)

HOLMES

It was beautiful, Watson. He fell into my trap like a Bengal tiger falling into a Shikari's pit!

WATSON

It *was* Moran?

HOLMES

Moriarty's chief executioner. He would of course send no one but the finest marksman in Europe.

MRS. HUDSON

Marksman—executioner—what does Mr. Holmes have in store for me next I wonder. A cannon blasting through the walls, or a murderer hanging by his neck from the window?

HOLMES

I'd rather prefer the latter, I think. There's a good clean sound to the cracking of a neck.

MRS. HUDSON

I shall have to try it one of these days. (*exits*)

HOLMES

(*to* GREGG)

Come in, come in. Sit down and tell us your problem, Captain. Or is it Lieutenant?

GREGG

Captain? Lieutenant?—What makes you think I'm in the army at all for that matter?

HOLMES

Come, come, your profession isn't hard to perceive—
Your manner, your bearing—
The very clothes you're wearing—
—that handkerchief tucked in your sleeve—
A military custom, I believe?

Of course you're an officer—
—Sandhurst, am I right?
And you're too young for a major
And so I should gauge you're
A captain.

GREGG

Well, I'll be—

HOLMES

Quite.

GREGG

Sir, I'm amazed!

HOLMES

You show surprise?
And yet the facts are there before your very eyes.
And it's so simple,
Sublimely simple,

If you learn not just to see but to observe.
Put your brain to work, not just the optic nerve.
If you put your mind to use
You will find the most abstruse
Becomes so simple.

WATSON

Oh yes, so simple
Just as simple as a simple thing can be.

HOLMES

And it's hardly very hard
To see he's in the palace guard.

WATSON

Oh no, it's simple as A B C.

GREGG

Now wait a minute! How did you know that I was in the palace guard?

HOLMES

My dear Captain
The line of your sunburn—straight across your brow.
No cap with a visor
Makes that mark, and I, sir,
Ask what type of headgear could possibly do that?
—a brimless bearskin hat!

Now who wears a busby?
You answer that and then
All other suppositions you discard—

Just guardsmen—and then only when
On duty in the palace yard!

GREGG

Well, I'll be bound!

HOLMES

Does it astound?
What other possible solution could be found?
It's all so simple,
Absurdly simple.
Why do people always fail to realize
That it's not enough to merely use their eyes?
They keep going 'round half-blind
Never using what's behind!

WATSON

You see it's simple

GREGG

Oh yes, it's simple

WATSON and GREGG

However difficult it might at first appear

HOLMES

And it isn't hard to place
There's a woman in the case—

WATSON and GREGG

Oh no it's simple
So very simple
It's as simple—

WATSON

Now Holmes, look here—
How on earth could you know there's a woman involved in his case?

HOLMES

The way I know we are about to have a visitor.

WATSON

Visitor?

HOLMES

A man — eleven stone — nearly seventy inches in height — and a heavy phlegmatic tread which could only belong —— to that senior member of our noble police force — (*flinging door open*) — Do come in, Inspector Lestrade.

LESTRADE

(*entering*)

Holmes, I've been waiting in that empty warehouse for four hours as you said, and he never turned up!

HOLMES

No matter. You played your part magnificently. Before detailing your brilliant strategy to you may I present my client, Captain —

GREGG

Robert Gregg.

HOLMES

Of the celebrated Coldstream Guards.

WATSON

Coldstream?

GREGG

How the devil did you know that?

WATSON

John Watson — 5th Northumberland Fusiliers.

GREGG

How 'do.

HOLMES

Your admirable modesty was defeated by the Egyptian scarab hanging from your watch chain. It speaks eloquently of your regiment's recent service in the Sudan.

LESTRADE

Hmpf! Not much of a trick to that.

HOLMES

You, of course, observed it too.

LESTRADE

The moment I entered.

HOLMES

As you will these curious bullets fired from the assassin's gun.

LESTRADE

Oh yes—yes, of course, I— (*examining bullets*) Holmes, what's curious about them?

HOLMES

My dear Inspector, surely it is obvious to you that—A snake!

LESTRADE, WATSON, and GREGG

A snake?

HOLMES

Dr. Roylott murdered his niece by putting a poison snake through the ventilator of her room. It's the only possible answer. Watson, be a good fellow, and send off another telegram—this time to the Surrey police. Now, as to these bullets—

WATSON

Another telegram? Holmes! How did you know I sent a telegram today?

HOLMES

Your shoes, dear chap, your shoes.

(WATSON *begins to examine his shoes.*)

LESTRADE

Shoes? Telegrams? Snakes? What's all that got to do with —

HOLMES

Another case entirely, Inspector.
Now the bullets are the work of Von Herder of Berlin,
Each as finely cut as any gem.
So your captive's clearly then
One of Moriarty's men
For Von Herder makes his masterpiece exclusively for them.

(*to* WATSON, *who is still examining his shoes*)

No, no,
Not the toe,
The heel of your slipper!
You'll note a trace of clay there, the color of a kipper.
That hue
Is my clue
And it makes the case complete
For such clay is only found
Where they're digging up the ground
At the doorway to the post office on Wigmore Street.

WATSON

Holmes!

HOLMES

(*to* GREGG)

—And as for you, sir, as far as I can see
The reason for your nervousness can only be one of three:
Either a mortal threat,
Or a very pressing debt,
Or the utterly inhuman
Machinations of a woman
Who is possibly toying
At destroying your career.
Is it she, or money, or terror brings you here?

Now from your bravery tonight it would surely appear
That if anything at all it isn't violence you fear,
And you gave that so-called beggar so much money that it's
clearly
The last alternative,
And positive
I am
When I say,
"Cherchez
la femme!"

GREGG

Why, sir, you're right.

LESTRADE

A child could do it.

WATSON

Once you get the knack there's really nothing to it.

GREGG

Why it's so simple!
Absurdly simple!

WATSON, GREGG, and LESTRADE

It's as obvious as two and two make four.

HOLMES

Rudimentary deduction, nothing more.

WATSON

Though at first we were impressed

LESTRADE

We see now that at its best

WATSON, GREGG, and LESTRADE

It's all so simple.

HOLMES

It's more than simple—
It's the very essence of simplicity!

WATSON and GREGG

No, we cannot disagree

LESTRADE

For as any fool can see

WATSON, GREGG, and LESTRADE

It's all so simple!
Oh yes, it's simple!

GREGG

Simple!

WATSON

Easy!

LESTRADE

Nothing!

GREGG

Basic!

LESTRADE

Child's play!

WATSON

Plainly as evident as evidence can be!

HOLMES

It's—

(*searches for the right word*)

Elementary!

A matter so simple, my dear Inspector, that I would not insult your intelligence by detaining you here a moment longer.

LESTRADE

But the woman who's trying to—

HOLMES

Thank God we are protected by the Metropolitan Detective Police.

LESTRADE

Quite so. Quite so.

HOLMES

(*ushering* LESTRADE *to the door*)

Good day, Inspector.

LESTRADE

Good day, good day. (*exits*)

HOLMES

And now, my dear Captain, about this woman.

GREGG

Her name is — Irene Adler.

WATSON

The American actress?

GREGG

Yes. I sent her a number of letters that were I'm afraid rather —

HOLMES

Letters?

GREGG

You know how it is, old man. They insist that you tell them how much you care. A touch of poetry now and again. A few — rose petals — pressed in an envelope.

HOLMES

You have come here — to ask me — to recover love letters?

GREGG

Yes.

HOLMES

Soon they shall be asking me to look for lost children at the seashore.

GREGG

But sir, she has threatened to publish them.

HOLMES

My dear fellow. Your problem to me is a boring affair without the least intellectual challenge. I suggest a lawyer.

GREGG

But you don't understand. She'd go to any lengths to—

(HOLMES *picks up the assassin's bullets.*)

HOLMES

You know, Watson, there is genius in this. Who would expect to find gold-dipped bullets fired from an ordinary pistol?

WATSON

Amazing.

GREGG

I'm engaged to a very fine person now—Lady Frances Carfax, the daughter of the Earl of Rufton—

HOLMES

Unquestionably the work of Von Herder, but no doubt devised by Moriarty himself.

WATSON

No doubt.

GREGG

—If there were a breath of scandal before the wedding—

HOLMES

I should not be surprised if he were behind the recent slaying of the Dutch Ambassador.

WATSON

Possible.

GREGG

—my entire future would be ruined.

HOLMES

But why on earth would he do this *now*—to *me?* Unless—

2

GREGG

Mr. Holmes, please listen to me!

HOLMES

— to stop me — (*turning to* GREGG) — from something.

GREGG

I'm a desperate man!

(HOLMES *studies* GREGG *in a new light.*)

HOLMES

Where did you meet this woman?

GREGG

A party.

HOLMES

Whose?

GREGG

The Duke of Richmond's.

HOLMES

You spoke to her first, or she to you?

GREGG

I don't remember.

(HOLMES *pauses, then examines the bullets in his hand once more.*)

HOLMES

Without question, Moriarty. (*exits to the left*)

GREGG

Who — or what — is Moriarty?

WATSON

A former professor of mathematics, now head of a vast empire of crime.

GREGG

Do you think Mr. Holmes will take my case?

WATSON

My dear chap, I very much doubt it.

(HOLMES *enters.*)

HOLMES

I'll take your case.

GREGG

Mr. Holmes, if you knew how much this means—

HOLMES

Yes, yes, I know. Where can you be reached tomorrow?

GREGG

I'll be on duty at the palace most of the day. There are gifts for the queen coming in from all over the world. For us that means checking passes—escorting delivery men up and down those interminable stairs—

HOLMES

Very well, I'll send you a message there tomorrow. Good night.

GREGG

Good night, sir.—Dr. Watson—

WATSON

Good night.

(GREGG *picks up his hat and gloves, then turns back to* WATSON.)

GREGG

5th Northumberland, eh?

WATSON

Oh yes, I picked up a Jezail bullet in my—

HOLMES

Good night! (GREGG *exits.* HOLMES *starts quickly to dress.*) I believe we may profit by the captain's callow behavior.

WATSON

Come now, Holmes. A young man—a beautiful actress—surely it was a human error.

HOLMES

Human error—how I despise that term. The mind of each man is a potentially perfect machine.

WATSON

There are also the glands.

HOLMES

Ah yes. A fact well known to Professor Moriarty who has used female agents in at least two previous crimes.

WATSON

You think the actress and the Professor?—

HOLMES

I think it is possible, Watson. But I shall put Miss Adler to a more conclusive test tonight.

WATSON

What sort of test?

HOLMES

I shall make her a generous offer for the letters. Her acceptance will indicate common blackmail. Her refusal—that would be something else again.

WATSON

If you'd like some help—

HOLMES

My dear fellow, I wouldn't dream of it. The backstage of a theatre is hardly the place for a respectable widower like yourself. Tawdry women rushing about half naked without the least particle of shame, some actually—(*picking up a thin volume from the chair*)—ah, Baudelaire! Illuminating description of the hallucinatory effects of hashish. I envy you this evening, Watson.

WATSON

Holmes—

HOLMES

Yes?

WATSON

I've read Baudelaire.

HOLMES

(*handing* WATSON *his hat*)

With luck we can make the final curtain.

Blackout

(*In the darkness we hear a series of pistol shots*)

Lights come up on . . .

ACT I

SCENE 2

TIME: *Later that night.*

SCENE: *The stage of the Theatre Royal where a chorus line of* GIRLS, *dressed as American Indians are seen performing a tribal dance.*

GIRLS

(*Sing*)

On the western prairies
When the Indians have taken to the warpath
And the western farmers
Badly need a helping hand to save the day,
Who's the one they call
When the arrows fall
Who's the one the settlers always pray
Will come to the rescue?

(IRENE ADLER *enters.*)

IRENE

Why it's
Buffalo Belle,
Buffalo Belle,
Queen of the wild, wild West.

How she can ride
How she can rope
But shootin's what she does best.

Iroquois, Apache, Seminole,

And even Sioux
Wisely lie low inside o' their wigwams.

They won't come out
While she's about
So when evil days you fall upon
You have only got to call upon
Buffalo Belle,
Buffalo Belle,
Queen of the wild, wild, West.

GIRLS

Buffalo Belle,
Buffalo Belle,
Queen of the wild, wild West.

How she can ride
How she can rope
But shootin's what she does best.

Iroquois, Apache, Seminole,
And even Sioux
Wisely lie low inside o' their wigwams.

IRENE

They won't come out
While she's about
So when evil days you fall upon
You have only got to call upon

IRENE and GIRLS

Buffalo Belle,
Buffalo Belle,
Queen of the wild, wild West.

(*After the number,* IRENE *and the* GIRLS *take their curtain calls*)

ACT I

SCENE 3

TIME: *The same.*

SCENE: *Backstage of the Theatre Royal, including a cutaway of* IRENE'S *dressing room.*

Friends and WELL-WISHERS *are waiting for* IRENE *outside her dressing room door. Some are sipping champagne, which* DAISY, *a maid, distributes. A flying bridge can be seen where* TWO STAGE-HANDS *are pulling up a long piece of hemp from the stage floor.*

IRENE *enters from left. There is a flurry of applause and exclamations of praise from the* WELL-WISHERS.

FIRST WELL-WISHER

Irene! Enchanting, my dear!

SECOND WELL-WISHER

How wonderful!

THIRD WELL-WISHER

Superb performance!

IRENE

Thank you, darlings, thank you.

(*A* FOURTH WELL-WISHER *hands her a glass of champagne.*)

FOURTH WELL-WISHER

A toast! A toast from the leading lady!

FIRST WELL-WISHER

Yes, yes! A toast!

SECOND WELL-WISHER

Quiet please for the toast!

(IRENE *lifts a champagne glass as* WELL-WISHERS *quiet down.*)

IRENE

To the downfall of all suffragettes—who would have us women gain a parcel of rights, and thereby lose a dynasty of privilege.

(*Hearty laughter from* WELL-WISHERS, *and cries of "Here, here!" "Well done!" etc.* HOLMES *now turns around, revealing himself and* WATSON *among the* WELL-WISHERS. *He raises a champagne glass.*)

HOLMES

And to crime—which may soon gain a parcel of profits for a very skillful practitioner. (WELL-WISHERS *become silent, as* IRENE *turns to* HOLMES.) Sherlock Holmes at your service, madam. Shall we talk in private?

(HOLMES *strides into the dressing room.* WATSON *follows.* WELL-WISHERS *begin buzzing at the mention of* HOLMES'S *name.*)

IRENE

I'll see you all later at the party, darlings. (*The* WELL-WISHERS *start to melt away.* IRENE *hesitates, then follows* HOLMES *and* WATSON *into the dressing room.*) To what do I owe this pleasure, Mr. Holmes?

HOLMES

I shall not waste time in the suburbs of the matter. I am here representing Captain Robert Gregg of the Coldstream Guards.

IRENE

Robert Gregg—that does sound familiar.

HOLMES

It should be *quite* familiar, madam.

IRENE

Of course! The young man who wanted his letters back. He did make a rather bad scene, I'm afraid, so I really had to turn him down. Besides, I don't believe in giving men a gratuitous sense of security.

HOLMES

It need not be gratuitous, madam. My client offers you fifty pounds for the letters. I advise you to take it while the offer remains.

IRENE

Does he value his letters so cheaply?

HOLMES

Very well, one hundred pounds. Bring the letters 'round to my flat at 221B Baker Street. Don't bother coming up. Just leave them with the woman downstairs. She'll have your money.

WATSON

But if you feel like coming up—

HOLMES

Come along, Watson.

(*They exit dressing room.* IRENE *follows.*)

IRENE

Wait—one moment, Mr. Holmes. You have made me a generous offer. But I will be more generous than that. You may tell your client I will *give* him his letters as a wedding gift—on the pages of the *Pall Mall Gazette.* The doorman will get you a cab, darling. (*exits into dressing room*)

HOLMES

Hypothesis confirmed. Miss Adler is not a simple blackmailer, but indeed may be connected to a larger crime, perhaps to the Moriarty group itself.

WATSON

What a pity. Such a very attractive woman.

HOLMES

That is quite irrelevant, Watson. The loveliest woman I ever knew murdered both her children for their insurance money. Come, we shall enlist the aid of our most dependable agents.

(They exit as the lights dim, except for a spotlight which hits the TWO STAGEHANDS *on the flying bridge.)*

FIRST STAGEHAND

Report to Professor Moriarty at once. Tell him that despite our endeavors, Sherlock Holmes has taken the case.

Blackout

ACT I

SCENE 4

TIME: *Early the next morning.*

SCENE: *An alley in Baker Street. In the darkness we see what appears to be a silhouette of* HOLMES. *As lights come up we perceive that it is not* HOLMES, *but* WIGGINS, *the leader of the* BAKER STREET IRREGULARS, *who wears a ragged version of the Holmesian costume.*

HOLMES *and* WATSON *enter swiftly, and walk up to* WIGGINS.

HOLMES

Mr. Wiggins!

WIGGINS

Sir! (*snaps to attention and salutes*)

HOLMES

I strongly recommend a change in costume.

WIGGINS

Yes, sir! (*removes his deerstalker cap*)

HOLMES

Are they about?

WIGGINS

About and at your service, sir!

HOLMES

You may assemble them.

(WIGGINS *whistles a shrill signal, and almost at once he is surrounded by the* BAKER STREET IRREGULARS, *a group of ragged urchins who stand in exaggerated postures of attention. He quickly calls off the roll and the* IRREGULARS *in turn answer to their respective names.)*

WIGGINS

Duckbellows! — Macipper! — Nipper! — Chauncey Weatherbee Perkins the Third! (*to* HOLMES) The Baker Street division of the metropolitan detective police force stands all present and correct, *sir!*

HOLMES

Stand easy! Gentlemen, I've a little job for you — (*The* IRREGULARS *cheer wildly.*) *With* your permission! (*a pause of silence*) I shall ask you to assist me in removing a packet of letters from the home of a woman in Serpentine Lane.

WIGGINS

(*to* IRREGULARS)

We're to pinch a batch of dear-Johnnies out of some doxie's lodgin's. Got it?

WIGGINS and IRREGULARS

Leave it to us, guv,
Leave it to us!

WIGGINS

Say the word and it's as good as done.

IRREGULARS

It's done!

MACIPPER

What do you need, guv?

NIPPER

Lookin' for speed, guv?

WIGGINS

For if it's speed you need
To do the deed

IRREGULARS

We'll do it on the run.

WIGGINS and IRREGULARS

Just name your fancy
And though it may be chancy
We'll fill the bill without a fuss

DUCKBELLOWS

And when no other blokes'll touch it,
Not for money nor for love

WIGGINS and IRREGULARS

Leave it to us, guv!
Leave it to us!

(IRREGULARS *end song with a burst of wild enthusiasm.* HOLMES *watches with cool distaste.*)

HOLMES

Your response is heartwarming, but there will be no "pinching" involved.

WIGGINS

Then how do we get the letters, sir?

HOLMES

You will merely toss a smoke rocket into the woman's bedroom window. She will assume there is a fire, and rush without thinking to save her valued possessions. I shall attend to the rest.

WIGGINS

We sends up the smoke, and *he* does the pinchin'. Got it?

WIGGINS and IRREGULARS

You can depend, guv.
Right to the end.
Everything is safely in the bag.

PERKINS

What have you got, guv?
Tell us the plot, guv,

WIGGINS

And in a shot
We'll do the lot

WIGGINS and IRREGULARS

Although we're not
The ones to brag.

WIGGINS

Give us an inkling

DUCKBELLOWS

And in a twinkling

WIGGINS and IRREGULARS

It's done and there's nothing to discuss!
For if you can't do it yourself
Then by the blinking saints above
Leave it to us, guv,
Leave it to us.

HOLMES
(after a pause)
Are they quite finished?

WIGGINS
Finished and ready for further instructions, sir!

HOLMES
You will receive the rest of your instructions at ten o'clock this morning, in Serpentine Lane.

WIGGINS
All troops report, four bells, Serpentine Lane! Got it!
(The IRREGULARS *take deep breaths, as though they are about to bellow forth.)*

HOLMES
One moment! *(The* IRREGULARS *freeze.)* My dear Watson, I've been meaning to speak to you about the Roylott affair— *(*HOLMES *and* WATSON *exit.)*

WIGGINS and IRREGULARS
(starting in a whisper, then growing in loudness)
Leave it to us, guv,
Leave it to us!
Your every little wish is our command.
Truer than true, guv,
We'll see you through, guv.
Give us a clue
And we will do
Whatever you
May have in hand.
We'll do our all, sir.
At your beck 'n' call, sir.
We'll give you satisfaction plus!
(Dance)

Leave it to us, guv
Leave it to us
Say the word and it's as good as . . .

(*Dance*)

If you need an 'elping 'and
To give that little extra shove
Give us a go, guv.

WIGGINS

We give satisfaction.

IRREGULARS

So, guv,

WIGGINS

Put us into action!

WIGGINS and IRREGULARS

'Oo you goin' to trust
To 'elp you keep the peace?

WIGGINS

Surely not the London Metropolitan Police!

WIGGINS and IRREGULARS

Trust the Irregulars
Just the Irregulars

SOLO LINES

Wiggins — Duckbellows — Nipper — Perkins — and Macipper

WIGGINS and IRREGULARS

The Baker Street Irregulars!
That's us!
That's us!

That's us!
That's us!
That's us!

Blackout

ACT I

Scene 5

TIME: *The same morning.*

SCENE: *The sitting room of* IRENE ADLER'S *rented house in St. John's Wood. At left, a door and a window facing the street. Upstage, a fireplace and a door leading to other rooms. At right, a pair of French doors open out to a garden, where there is a little stone bench.*

IRENE *is sitting on the sofa in a breathtaking dressing gown.*

DAISY, *the maid, enters from the hallway, fully dressed for traveling. She carries a valise and three books.*

IRENE

I see you found them.

DAISY

Honestly, ma'am, I don't know *why* you want to read such things. *The Case of the Sussex Vampire*—drank human blood, or so it appeared . . . *The Man with the Twisted Lip*—all about an opium den . . . *The Adventure of the Engineer's Thumb*—chopped off by a butcher's cleaver . . . and to think they let them print such things.

IRENE

Why do you read them, Daisy?

DAISY

To see how far they would dare to go. See you at the show tonight, ma'am.

(DAISY *exits.* IRENE *picks up one of the books and begins to read.*)

IRENE

My analysis of Sherlock Holmes, by John Watson, M.D. Holmes is a master of disguise with a knowledge of science that is truly profound. He is well up on poisons generally. Knows nothing of practical gardening.

(*loud knocking at the door*)

WIGGINS

(*offstage*)

Open the door! Open up, ma'am! Quick! (IRENE *opens the door.* WIGGINS *and the* IRREGULARS *enter.*) A man's been hit by a carriage!

NIPPER

In front of your house!

MACIPPER

I think he's some kind of priest!

WIGGINS

He's moanin' and groanin' like a bloke wot's croakin'!

IRENE

Help me bring him inside.

WIGGINS

Good idea! (*While* IRENE *and the* IRREGULARS *exit,* WIGGINS *remains onstage and surveys the room. A few seconds later* IRENE *and the* IRREGULARS *return, all helping to carry* HOLMES, *who is disguised as an Anglican deacon. They place him on the sofa.*) Easy now, lads.

IRENE

Is he breathing?

WIGGINS

I just seen him twitchin' a bit.

IRENE

I wonder if smelling salts . . .

WIGGINS

I think leeches might do it.

IRREGULARS

Leeches! That's it! Somebody get leeches!

IRENE

No! Get a doctor—quickly!

WIGGINS

Yes, ma'am, a doctor! C'mon, lads! (*They exit.*)

HOLMES

What's happened? Where . . .

IRENE

You've had an accident.

HOLMES

Accident?

IRENE

Everything's going to be all right. I've sent for a doctor.

HOLMES

Oh yes—I remember now. Carriage—wheels rattling on the cobblestones—coming so fast—

IRENE

Sssshhh! Try to get some rest. Are you comfortable, Reverend?

HOLMES

Yes, quite comfortable, thank you.

IRENE

I'll get you a cup of tea.

HOLMES

One moment — my dear.

IRENE

Yes?

HOLMES

With milk and sugar, if you don't mind.

IRENE

Of course.

HOLMES

And hot. I like it very hot.

(*Smoke begins to pour into the room.*)

IRENE

My word!

HOLMES

What is it? — The chimney stopped up — or something worse? —

IRENE

I think you'd best go into the garden. (HOLMES *rises from sofa, and stumbles through billows of smoke to the garden.* IRENE *runs to front door, and calls into the street:*) You! Young man!

(WIGGINS *pokes his head in the doorway.*)

WIGGINS

Yes, ma'am.

IRENE

Get the fire brigade! Please hurry!

WIGGINS

Righto! (*exits*)

HOLMES

(*calling from garden*)

Is everything all right?

IRENE

Yes, everything's fine. (*picks up a scrapbook and birdcage, and takes them to* HOLMES *in the garden*) Would you mind very much?

HOLMES

No, not at all. (IRENE *returns to the sitting room, and starts to open a secret wall safe. In the garden,* HOLMES *riffles the scrapbook furiously in search of the letters. When the wall safe is open,* IRENE *removes a catchall box containing mementos and letters. She takes them to* HOLMES *in the garden, then returns to the sitting room, looking for further objects to save. Suddenly* IRENE *stops in her tracks, realizing something is wrong. She looks back through the garden doors, in time to see the Reverend poring over her papers and letters.* HOLMES *catches her eye, and tries to cover his act by lifting a single rose from the box of letters, and sniffing it.*) How beautiful!

IRENE

(*with an edge to her voice*)

You may come in now, Reverend.

HOLMES

But the fire—

IRENE

It's under control—(*steps into the garden, and takes the box of letters out of his hands*)—and thank you so much for minding these. (*Waving the letters under his nose, she leads him back to the sitting room where the smoke has all but vanished. She sings:*)

Letters,
Letters,
I do love letters—

HOLMES

Love letters, my dear?

IRENE

Don't you love letters?
A word from afar
From someone who's dear,
A line from a friend—
Oh, this one you've *got* to hear!
(*striking a regal pose, she reads*)
Dear Miss Adler,

My royal heart is in your hands.
My royal fate is in your hands.
I am unworthy and unfit,
But say you'll take me and my little
Balkan state is in your hands!

For
My line needs new blood—
It's much too refined.
Red blood with blue blood,
The two bloods combined.
My blood with your blood—
The best blood I could find!
Signed,
Wilhelm, King of Bohemia,
Dying of love—and anemia!

[2] Fritz Weaver as Sherlock Holmes, Peter Sallis as Dr. Watson, and Inga Swenson as Irene Adler in Holmes's Baker Street flat; Act I, Scene 7.

[3] Inga Swenson as Irene Adler and Fritz Weaver as Sherlock Holmes disguised for their journey through the London underworld; Act I, Scene 8.

[4] Martin Gabel as Professor Moriarty aboard Moriarty's yacht; Act I, Scene 9.

Letters,
Letters,
I do love letters—
A note from abroad,
A card from Brazil—
Now isn't that nice?
Not that—that's a bill!
Letters,
Letters—
A letter from home
Here's one from *Wyoming!?*
Oh yes, of course—him!

(*as a cowboy*)

Pardon my writin',
Pardon my script,
Pardon the place where the inkwell slipped!

Miss Irene Adler, I loves you.
I bless the shinin' day when you was born!
I'm worth two million dollars
And natcherly it follers
If you say "yes" then all my dough is yourn!
That day I saw you there in the the-at-er,
I swore that I would marry you or none!
So please say you'll select me,
For if'n you reject me
I swear I'll blow my head off with my
Custom-tailored,
Gold-plated,
Pearl-handled,
Diamond-studded
Solid platinum gun!
Signed, Bill
P.S. I loves you still.

Letters,
Letters,
I so love letters!
Mail from afar,
A card from an aunt—
Oh this you should see!
Oh no, no you can't!
Letters,
Letters—
Here's one from a fan.
Oh my, this is fun!
Here's one from a man—
And this one's from London!
You English aren't as cool as you like to appear, Reverend.
Listen here, Reverend . . .

(*reads with exaggerated emotion*)

You are my ecstasy, my worship, my wonder!
If you should spurn me, my heart would burst asunder!
One word from you alone can make me or break me!
Take me, Irene, I beg!
Signed,
Captain Robert . . .

Isn't this the name you've been waiting for, Mr. Holmes?

Gregg!!!

You really had me fooled, Mr. Holmes. Your disguise is perfect. But when I saw these letters in your hands, I realized that only the great Sherlock Holmes could have made me reveal them. (*offers letters to* HOLMES) Here—you've earned them.

(HOLMES *pulls himself up to full height and drops the ministerial accent from his voice.*)

HOLMES

The fact that you offer them, madam, makes my obtaining them

quite unnecessary. And thank you very much for the entertainment. I don't get to the theatre very often.

(HOLMES *exits.* IRENE *laughs, then starts to put the letters back in the secret wall compartment. As she is doing this, a little man with a satchel enters from another room.* IRENE *gasps in fright.*)

BAXTER

I did not mean to alarm you, madam. I am Dr. Baxter of Edgware Road. I knocked at the front, but there was no answer, so I came through the kitchen. Where is the injured party?

IRENE

(*relieved; she smiles*)

I'm afraid he's gone, Doctor. He responded miraculously to my treatment.

BAXTER

Splendid! I welcome all the assistance I can get—

Lights fade out

ACT I

SCENE 6

TIME: *A few hours later.*

SCENE: *Outside the Buckingham Palace Gate, where tourists and sightseers are gawking at the stiffly standing sentries.*

CAPTAIN GREGG, *in full uniform, crosses from stage left to the cadence of martial music. A* MAN *enters running, also from left, and catches up to* GREGG *at center.*

MAN

Captain Robert Gregg?

(GREGG *stops. All action freezes.*)

GREGG

What is your business, sir?

MAN

(*showing card*)

McNally—*Daily Globe.* I've been assigned to cover your forthcoming wedding to Lady Frances Carfax.

GREGG

This is hardly the place . . .

MAN

A pity if something unforeseen should happen first.

GREGG

What the devil do you mean by that?

(*The* MAN *takes a letter from his pocket, and reads aloud:*)

MAN

"My beloved Irene; you are my ecstasy, my worship, my wonder . . ."

GREGG

Where did you get this?

MAN

There are twenty-two more where it came from, Captain.

GREGG

How much do you want for them?

MAN

Ahh! Did I say anything about money?

Tourists' action resumes. Lights fade out

ACT I

SCENE 7

TIME: *Later that day.*

SCENE: *The Baker Street flat.*

HOLMES *is seated on floor, playing his violin in a mood of black, brooding anger.* WATSON, *who is writing memoirs at his desk, appears concerned over* HOLMES*'s condition.*

WATSON

What a lovely night for a stroll.

HOLMES

By all means take one!

WATSON

Holmes, I would not let a trivial thing like the Adler letters—

HOLMES

Miss Adler and her confounded letters could not be further from my mind.

WATSON

I am sure another case will come along before—

HOLMES

—before you drive me to insanity with your constant chatter?

WATSON

Quite.

HOLMES

There is no case, no clue, no crime of the slightest importance to me now. Everything is bleak and dismal. (*at window*) Look at that fog drifting meaninglessly down there. All life is dreary and commonplace. Is there no escape? (*crosses to fireplace*)

WATSON

Holmes! You really must—

HOLMES

You really must spare me your sanctimonious sermons!

(WATSON, *unable to continue writing, rises from desk and goes to window.*)

WATSON

Holmes, there's a carriage outside.

HOLMES

Two visitors on the stairs—a man—Lestrade—a woman—willful, determined, and somewhat below the age of forty, I should think. (*a knocking at the door*) Well, show the lady in, Watson.

(WATSON *opens the door.* IRENE *and* LESTRADE *barge in.*)

IRENE

Arrest that man!

LESTRADE

She insisted upon this, Holmes.

HOLMES

On what charge, madam?

IRENE

Fraud, deception, torts, encroachment, vile misrepresentation—and theft!

HOLMES

Theft?

IRENE

Having failed to trick me with your disguise, you returned while I was away and stole what you could not obtain by deceit.

HOLMES

Your letters, they're gone?

IRENE

You know perfectly well, they're gone.

HOLMES

Miss Adler, I did not steal your letters, although I admit I attempted to.

LESTRADE

Attempted theft?

HOLMES

Yes, yes, I confess to it now.

LESTRADE

Sorry, Holmes.

HOLMES

For until ten twenty-two this morning I believed Miss Adler to have criminal intent. She does not, but I have carelessly allowed her letters to fall into the hands of a sinister organization.

LESTRADE

What sinister organization?

HOLMES

Madam, if you will co-operate with me now, I shall try to recover your letters, and perhaps stop a crime that may endanger the honor of England.

LESTRADE

Holmes! What crime are you talking about?

HOLMES

The one that has no doubt crossed your mind, Inspector.

LESTRADE

Oh!

HOLMES

Yes — pray, keep me informed of your progress. (*ushers* LESTRADE *toward the door*)

LESTRADE

Yes, yes, I'll do that, I certainly will, I —

HOLMES

Good day, Inspector!

LESTRADE

Good day! (*exits*)

HOLMES

Now then, would you please describe all persons who have been in your house within the past twenty-four hours.

IRENE

You mean the suspects?

HOLMES

Yes—all persons you remember.

IRENE

As I don't have a butler, it must be the maid. She is approximately—

HOLMES

We may dispense with that twenty-five-year-old red-haired girl who left to visit her sailor in Brighton at six minutes after ten while the letters were still intact. I noticed one or two clues in your house. Continue.

IRENE

There was the deacon.

HOLMES

Oh yes.

IRENE

However, I cannot suspect that kindly old man who cared so little about himself that he left before medical aid arrived.

HOLMES

Are you quite certain you're not overlooking someone? A friend, a— Did you say medical aid?

IRENE

Dr. Baxter of Edgware Road. I sent the lad to fetch that very fine doctor for you, Mr. Holmes, as you will discover when you get his bill.

HOLMES

My dear Watson, would you be so good as to step 'round the corner to the Medical Society, and inquire about a Dr. Baxter of Edgware Road.

WATSON

Of course.

HOLMES

I believe we shall find that he does not exist, except in the employ of Professor Moriarty.

WATSON

Oh? What makes you think that?

HOLMES

The curious fact that Miss Adler sent the Irregulars to fetch him.

WATSON

But you told them in advance not to fetch anyone.

HOLMES

That, my dear Watson, is the curious fact.

WATSON

I see . . . I think.

(WATSON *exits. There is a considerable silence as* HOLMES *wonders how to cope with his female guest.*)

HOLMES

Cigar, Miss Adler?

IRENE

Not now. (*Wanders around the flat as* HOLMES *busies himself at the laboratory table. She picks up an object covered by a glass bell.*) A tooth from the hound of the Baskervilles?

HOLMES

A fang from the giant rat of Sumatra.

IRENE

Have you ever kissed a woman, Mr. Holmes?

HOLMES

Several times in the course of investigations.

IRENE

Did you find the experience pleasurable?

HOLMES

The labial contact was pleasant, and induced a faint quickening of the pulse, and a flushing of tissue in the neck and facial areas which ultimately subsided. It was akin to — La Grippe.

IRENE

You of course do not believe in love.

HOLMES

I believe that *people* believe in love. Take the case of Lemuel Dundas and his adoring wife who choked him to death by shoving a set of false teeth down his gullet.

IRENE

I am sure she loved him very much.

HOLMES

So she said on the gallows — just before flashing that brave toothless smile.

I have waited in vain
For someone to explain
What love conceivably can offer
The cerebral type of man,
But no one ever has
And no one ever will
For no one ever can —
But, ah!

The cold, clear world of the intellect
Is the world that I revere.
In the pure, dry air of the scientist
I am in my proper sphere.
To illumine what was dark
With a spark of cerebral electricity—
There's felicity!
From a fragment, to construct
The comprehensive whole—
There's nectar for the soul!

From the thick, black cloak of a mystery
To deduce the why and how.
Just a loaf of bread and a cryptogram
This were paradise enow.
With the power of the mind
To find what a foe has concealed
With dev'lish care—
There's joy!
There's happiness!
And to spare!

I have waited in vain
For someone to explain
What love conceivably can offer
The cerebral type of man
But no one ever has
And no one ever will—
For no one ever can.
(*faces her challengingly*)

IRENE

Love is a delicate subject
On which I have little to say.
And yet there are difficult subjects
I'd gladly debate half the day.

Finding words for spring
Is no easy thing
Still I'm sure I'd find a few.
What words could be right
To describe the night?
Somehow, I would find them too.
How can one explain
Love's sweet splendor
The most tender words won't do.
You must fall in love
Then you'll find that love
Will explain itself to you.

(*moves closer to him*)

The cold, clear world of the intellect, Mr. Holmes?

Should you want to praise
Lazy summer days
I could find a phrase or two.
As for love, mere words,
Though they're clever,
They'll just never, never do.
You must fall in love
Then you'll find that love
Will explain itself to you.

(HOLMES *and* IRENE *are standing very close to each other as* WATSON *enters.*)

WATSON

There *is* a Dr. Baxter on the Medical Society's records. He died four years ago.

HOLMES

Twelve hours — to prevent a crime so despicable it may eclipse the pillaging of Rheims.

WATSON

Can't you warn the authorities now?

HOLMES

Send a herd of elephants after a panther? He would only return by another route while the pachyderms were trampling insects miles away. I must find the professor myself—perhaps with the aid of one other. Miss Adler, would you take a risk for your letters?

IRENE

I could not care less for those letters now, but I think I would like the risk.

HOLMES

After your show tonight, you will play an extra performance—with me. We shall appear as members of the lower class, and journey through the underworld of London. Our purpose—to find Dr. Baxter of Edgware Road, our link to Professor Moriarty.

IRENE

Our link.

HOLMES

Watson, would you be good enough to see Miss Adler to the theatre.

WATSON

It would be an extraordinary pleasure. Miss Adler—? (IRENE *turns to* WATSON) I would be interested in meeting one or two of your actress friends—for purely aesthetic reasons, of course—

(*Lights fade, except for a spotlight on* HOLMES's *makeup table.* HOLMES *sits at the table facing a mirror, and begins to disguise himself quickly and deftly.*)

HOLMES

Now—
Beard . . .
Heavy—
Hmmm—
Perhaps a little darker—
There!
Now for the eyes . . .
There!
And there!
Chin . . .
A touch of number nine—
Fine!
—Now, where in the devil is that spirit gum?—

(*Lights fade on* HOLMES *and come up on* IRENE *and* DAISY *in* IRENE'S *dressing room.*)

IRENE

Daisy!

DAISY

Yes, ma'am.

IRENE

What shall I wear?

DAISY

The red, ma'am?

IRENE

No, the blue.
No, that's hopeless.

DAISY

What about the mauve, ma'am?

IRENE

What—?

DAISY

The mauve with the bustle.

IRENE

Gorgeous—
On you.

DAISY

What!
With my derriere?

IRENE

I've simply got nothing to wear!

I was mad
To say yes
But I'm glad
Nonetheless.
What a night this is going to be!

There's a scent
There's a hum
Of adventure to come
What a night this is going to be!

Tonight's a night that's fraught with excitement!
Tonight—is a night meant
For me!
For tonight I'm with him!
Win or lose, sink or swim!
In or out, wrong or right—
What a night this is going to be!

(*Lights fade on* IRENE *and* DAISY *and come up on* HOLMES, *now joined by* WATSON.)

HOLMES

Watson.

WATSON

Yes?

HOLMES

How do I look?

WATSON

Dreadful!

HOLMES

Good!
Eyebrows . . .

WATSON

Eyebrows?

HOLMES

Yes or no?

WATSON

Well, I wouldn't—

HOLMES

Then I should.

So it's off to the hunt
In a few minutes' time—
What a night this is going to be!

Now at last I confront
That Napoleon of crime!
What a night this is going to be!

Tonight there'll be an intimate party
For just Moriarty
And me—
And Miss Adler of course—
Perhaps I should feel remorse—
For she can't know just quite
What a night this is going to be!
(*Lights come up on* IRENE *and* DAISY.)

IRENE

Somehow it is strange
I'm not afraid of all the
Dangers of tonight.

DAISY

Oh ma'am, I know you ain't!
But as for me, I feel
I'm going to faint!

IRENE

Compared to what's in store
now
All the roles I played before
now
Seem so trite

HOLMES

It's just about complete

WATSON

By Jove, you look a treat

IRENE

Just to think that
He—
Puts his trust in
Me.
Who can know
How it may go?

HOLMES

Just to think that
She—
Puts her trust in
Me

Together we
Shall see
What we
Shall see—

I was mad
To say yes
But I'm glad
Nonetheless
What a night this is going to be!

Together we
Shall see
What we
Shall see—

She was mad
To say yes
But I'm glad
Nonetheless
What a night this is going to be!

WATSON

Oh, Holmes, you are the one!
I've never had such fun!
There's going to be
Skulduggery
Before the night is done!

DAISY

What a night
This night
Is going to be!

IRENE

There's a dash
There's a dare
In the air
Everywhere!
What a night this is going to be!

HOLMES

There's a dash
There's a dare
In the air
Everywhere!
What a night this is going to be!

DAISY

Just look at you! oh my!
Miss Adler, I could die!
I swear I'm so beside myself
I think I'm going to cry!

WATSON

What a night
This night
Is going to be!

IRENE and HOLMES

Tonight's a night that's fraught with excitement
Tonight is a night meant for me!

WATSON

So it's on with the case!

IRENE

And there's no time to spare

HOLMES

So it's off to the chase!

DAISY

Oh Miss Adler, take care!

HOLMES, WATSON, IRENE, and DAISY

Come what may!
Come what might!
What a night this is going to be!

(HOLMES *completes his disguise of a crude underworld character. He rises from the makeup table, which fades to black and crosses to* IRENE'*s dressing room. He knocks.* IRENE *comes to the door and looks at him blankly.*)

IRENE

Yes?

HOLMES

That will do very nicely, Miss Adler.

IRENE

(*now recognizing* HOLMES)

Oh God, that's good!

HOLMES

If at any time during the night, you should see the man who calls himself Dr. Baxter, kindly signal me by waving a white handkerchief over your head. (*She waves it wildly.*) With a trifle more restraint. And remember, from this moment on you are Mrs. Brasser Bates of Bethnal Green. Is that perfectly clear?

IRENE

As clear as a paneless window, love. And speakin' o' drafts, I feels a bit of a chill in the air — (*entwining her arm in his*) so if I holds on like a sailor's girl, it's warmth, not intimacy I'm seekin'. Mind, love?

HOLMES

Your "A's" are a trifle flat.

IRENE

'Ullo ducks.

HOLMES

'Ullo sweet.
My, you do look a treat!

IRENE and HOLMES

What a night this is going to be!

IRENE

Come on, give us a kiss.

HOLMES

What, in public like this?

IRENE and HOLMES

What a night this is going to be!
Tonight's a night just right for a blowout,
Tonight is just my cup o' tea!

IRENE

What a lark!

[5] The Baker Street Irregulars in a street scene prior to the Diamond Jubilee parade; Act II, Scene 1.

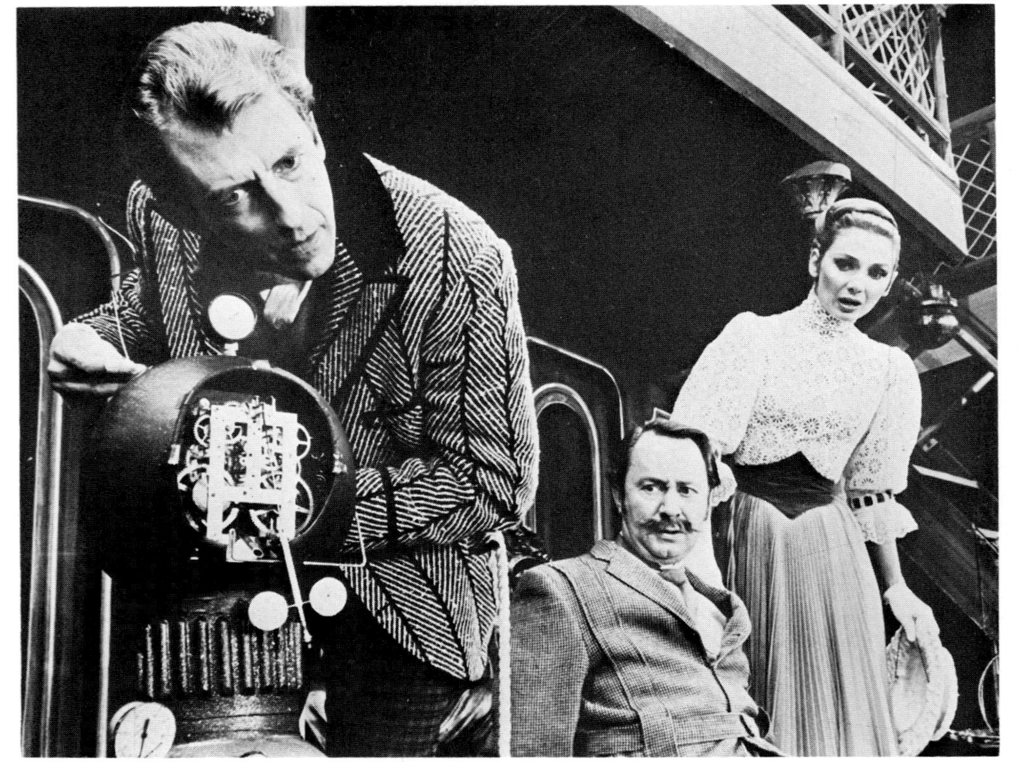

[6] Fritz Weaver as Sherlock Holmes neutralizes Professor Moriarty's "fantastic chronometer of death" while Peter Sallis as Dr. Watson and Inga Swenson as Irene Adler look on; Act II, Scene 2.

[7] Fritz Weaver as Sherlock Holmes contemplating Professor Moriarty's possible escape routes; Act II, Scene 3.

[8] Fritz Weaver as Sherlock Holmes and Martin Gabel as Professor Moriarty on the cliffs of Dover; Act II, Scene 4.

IRENE

Look out!

MURILLO

Run, Miss Adler!

(IRENE *runs off as the* THREE KILLERS *attack* MURILLO. *He puts up a valiant fight, but is eventually overpowered and killed. The* THREE KILLERS *exit.* IRENE *re-enters from the alley, and we realize that she has witnessed the killing. She hesitates a moment, then starts to follow the* KILLERS *off*)

Lights fade out

ACT I

SCENE 9

TIME: *Early the next morning.*

SCENE: *The deck and luxurious cabin of a private yacht tied up on the river Thames. The cabin, rich in eastern treasure, suggests exotic decadence. It contains a Buddha with incense burning at its feet. As lights come up slowly, the* THREE KILLERS *are seen standing guard on deck.*

BAXTER *and* GANG MEMBERS *appear on deck with* HOLMES *in tow. They conduct him roughly to the cabin below.*

HOLMES

(*still keeping his disguise as Brasser Bates*)

Aw right, aw right! No need to use yer maulees!

BAXTER

Sit down.

(HOLMES *sits, and looks around the cabin.*)

HOLMES

'Ere, what's this? A branch o' the British Muzeem?

(BAXTER *signals to the* GANG MEMBERS, *who begin to exit.*)

BAXTER

I'll be just outside, so mind you, no tricks.

HOLMES

Naw!

(BAXTER *exits.* HOLMES *finds an expensive cigar on a table, lights it, and sits back luxuriantly. There is the sound of an oriental gong.* HOLMES *sits up startled, and turns toward the Buddha, which revolves, revealing* PROFESSOR MORIARTY. *He is seated at a blackboard filled with mathematical formulae.)*

MORIARTY

(*studying* HOLMES)

You are an unknown quantity, Mr. Bates. A factor which never fails to intrigue me.

HOLMES

Just put two and two together, guv, and make sure the answer's writ in pounds sterling — for services rendered, of course.

MORIARTY

Yond Cassius has a lean and hungry look. That is Shakespeare, Mr. Bates.

HOLMES

Well fancy that!

MORIARTY

(*rising from blackboard, and crossing to a cage with tropical birds*)

Last night you undertook to harass and pursue certain intimate friends of mine. Why was that?

HOLMES

Well, follow the cubs to the lion, I always say.

MORIARTY

That is sometimes a one-way trail, Mr. Bates.

HOLMES

I think you'll open it up when you hears what I got to offer, guv.

MORIARTY

I am ablaze with curiosity. What services had you in mind?

HOLMES

I thought you'd never ask. I'm a proper fence. Some say the best in Her Majesty's Kingdom from Mersey Docks to Bristol Port.

MORIARTY

Why should that be of the slightest interest to me?

HOLMES

Why should the rain be of interest to flowers that bloom? Especially those in the Royal Gardens, eh guv?

MORIARTY

May I inquire as to the source of your peculiar supposition?

HOLMES

Now that's a long story, guv. There's a bloke up north named Percy Freen what knows a pickpocket named Harry Grale what knows a dress lodger called Minnie Brown what knows—(*dropping characterization and removing disguise*)—a very good friend of mine who is at this moment approaching with Dr. Watson and a large contingent of police. Good morning, Professor.

MORIARTY

O mighty Caesar! Dost thou lie so low? . . . You are thinner than I had imagined.

HOLMES

And you are exactly as I have imagined.

MORIARTY

How did you learn of my plans today?

HOLMES

You revealed them yourself by stealing Miss Adler's letters. They could only be used against Captain Gregg, and his job made it clear that the object of your plan was the palace.

MORIARTY

And as to details of my — late and lamented scheme?

HOLMES

I have analyzed four different methods of stealing the Queen's Diamond Jubilee gifts.

MORIARTY

There are five. Have you thought of the two reporters who arrive at the palace at the height of the parade?

HOLMES

A colleague is with them of course.

MORIARTY

A photographer — eager to capture for all posterity the glittering sight of the Jubilee gifts.

HOLMES

I presume that all three then enter the palace.

MORIARTY

With the aid of the good Captain Gregg, who believes he is doing nothing more evil than assisting three enterprising journalists. A minor infraction to be sure in exchange for his stimulating letters. At exactly nine forty-six they return to the palace yard, the photographer's satchel now bulging with two million pounds' worth of celebrated gems.

HOLMES

The stolen gems to be replaced by replicas, of course.

MORIARTY

Of course these would never fool an expert like you. But to call them merely replicas would hardly be appropriate. (*opens jewel box*) An emerald tiara from the Sultan of Mysore—a diamond solitaire from the Caliph of Persia.

HOLMES

Ah, beautiful. Made by Von Herder, naturally.

MORIARTY

Is there another?

HOLMES

Your escape from England of course to be effected by balloon.

MORIARTY

Directional.

HOLMES

Capacity?

MORIARTY

One hundred thousand cubic feet.

HOLMES

Electric propulsion?

MORIARTY

Engine by La Farge.

HOLMES

Maximum range?

MORIARTY

Shall we merely say it is enough to transport me far from this sceptered isle.

HOLMES

Ah, neat! It will go down in the annals of famous uncommitted crimes.

MORIARTY

Oh yes, you have found me, haven't you? And your agents are fetching the police. Well then, we must not keep them waiting.

(*Signals toward a corridor. Two* GANG MEMBERS *enter with* WATSON *in tow.*)

WATSON

They came to the flat this morning, Holmes. They said they were your men.

HOLMES

What have you done with —

MORIARTY

Your pigeon? His death was crude. (GANG MEMBERS *begin to tie* HOLMES *and* WATSON *into their chairs.*) But yours, Holmes, will be a work of art. (GANG MEMBERS *exit.* MORIARTY *unveils the time bomb, a gleaming instrument of dials, springs, and balance wheels.*) Observe Von Herder's masterpiece. A fantastic chronometer of death, which once begun cannot be touched without producing — detonation.

I shall miss you, Holmes,
For in truth we are fellow connoisseurs
And it grieves me, Holmes,
To eclipse such an intellect as yours.

I've enjoyed each thrust and parry
And riposte.
Yes, your genius was indeed a match for mine —
Almost.

I shall miss you, sir
I regret your reversion into dust.
Life is hard, dear Holmes,
And one does what one must.

Your demise ensures
The unobstructed birth
Of an empire that will
Circumscribe the earth!

The Jubilee gifts are a mere beginning. Two million pounds for the purchase of power. Through drugs, through lust, through secret cravings in the minds of men. And how they shall love me for my tolerance of their weaknesses! That is why I shall rise to my zenith—whilst you are blown to dust. (*triggers time bomb, which begins to tick*)

Ah! You can't know how profoundly
I shall miss you, Holmes,
'Though your death is essential to my schemes.
You must die, dear Holmes,
Yet as strange as it seems

I shall mourn
As I have never mourned before
When the stately Holmes of England
Is no more.

(MORIARTY *exits via the revolving Buddha.* HOLMES *and* WATSON *look at the time bomb, which seems to tick louder and louder as*)

Curtain falls

ACT II

SCENE 1

TIME: *Later that morning.*

SCENE: *A street in London where crowds are gathering to watch the Diamond Jubilee parade. There are vendors, including a flag vendor; some colorfully dressed guardsmen rushing to join their units; a few foreign visitors, including an East Indian couple and an* AMERICAN COUPLE, *who are taking pictures of everything in sight with their cameras. Three* GANG MEMBERS *are seen going toward the palace; one carries a large tripod camera.*

In the midst of all this, WIGGINS *is being lowered to the street in the Roof Space Box, a crudely constructed "lift" rigged with ropes and pulleys which is hoisted up and down by the* BAKER STREET IRREGULARS.

WIGGINS

Roof space!
Roof space!
Roof space for a shilling!
Oh the view is thrilling!
Roof space!
Roof space!

(*After being lowered to the street,* WIGGINS *leaps out of the box and hands the* IRREGULARS *signs and placards advertising roof space. The* AMERICAN COUPLE *walk by.*)

Here's a likely pair of colonials. (*to* AMERICAN COUPLE) I say, it's a shame.

AMERICAN MAN

What's a shame, fella?

WIGGINS

Shame you ain't goin' to see the parade.

AMERICAN MAN

We're headin' there right now.

WIGGINS

Well, I can see that you're not goin' to see nothing, are you? Not unless you got a particular fancy for the tops of soldiers' heads. Personally, I think if you've seen one fluffy hat, you've seen them all.

AMERICAN WOMAN

C'mawn, daddy — we gonna be late.

WIGGINS

Now if you *really* want to see the parade, go no farther. You're here!

If you want to see what there is to see,
If you want to 'ear what there is to 'ear,
If you want a view of the Diamond Jubilee parade,
Then with our aid
Go up on the blinkin' roof
And I will swear as it's gawd's own troof
You can see the route of the whole darn march
From 'ere to the Marble Arch.
Up there you can see all the Fusiliers,
The Coldstream Guards
And the Grenadiers —
Why you'll even see the Queen
I mean as clear as day.
But I must say
If you stay in the crowd below,
Though you may stand on your tippy-toe,
Oh you can try to peep,

You can try to peer,
But all you'll see is a policeman's rear!
On the roof above
Y' don't 'ave to push, y' don't 'ave to shove.
From a comfy seat you can see for blocks—
Cor! It's like the Royal Box!
To see all there is to see
Way up on the roof is the place to be—
And what's the total fare?
Just a bob for the chair
And we fly you there for free.

(*The* AMERICAN COUPLE *exit and* WIGGINS *tries to hawk roof space to numerous other passers-by.*)

WIGGINS

Gather 'round all. Fresh roof space. Roof space, miss? Roof space, sir? Form an orderly queue. (*Passers-by ignore him.*)

On the blinkin' tiles
You can see for miles and miles and miles.
You'll be sitting there so grand
And the Queen will wave her hand.
She'll say "My goodness me!
Way up on the roof is the place to be."
So c'mon now
A bob in the cup and
We hauls you up for free.

Roof space!
Roof space!
See the 'ole parade miss!
Don't you be afraid miss!
Roof space!
Roof space!

(*The* IRREGULARS *dance, causing a crowd to gather around and watch. When dance ends, crowd begins to disperse.*)

WIGGINS

All right! Who's goin' to be the first to buy roof space? (*spots a* FAT MAN *holding a coin up high*) Roof space?

FAT MAN

Yes!

WIGGINS

Lads!

(*The* IRREGULARS *cheer. Then they and* WIGGINS *escort the* FAT MAN *to the Roof Space Box in mock military formation. They are about to hoist him up when* IRENE *enters looking desperate. She recognizes the* IRREGULARS.)

IRENE

You! — You're the boys who helped carry him into my house!

WIGGINS

Who, us?

IRENE

Yes, you!

WIGGINS

I don't know what you're talkin' about, miss.

IRENE

Of course you know! You're the one I sent to get a doctor!

WIGGINS

You know what she's talkin' about, lads?

IRENE

Please listen to me! He's in trouble. He's been captured by the Moriarty gang. I followed him all through —

WIGGINS

Look! I don't know what you're on about, but I do know this. If he was in trouble, I'd be the first to know! So go beat your drum in some other parade, miss.

FAT MAN

Hey! What about me? I paid my shilling!

WIGGINS

Look to it, lads!

NIPPER

All together!

(They begin to hoist the Roof Space Box. IRENE *helps them pull the ropes while trying to get their attention.)*

IRENE

Boys, listen to me! You don't understand! His life is in danger! I want to help him. Please—

(As the FAT MAN *is hoisted up to the roof, the lights fade to black. A bird's eye view of the street now appears, and we see the Diamond Jubilee parade in all its splendor. Military music can be heard. After several regiments go by, Queen Victoria appears in her golden carriage, and the sound of cheering becomes overpowering as)*

Lights fade to black

ACT II

SCENE 2

TIME: *Several minutes later.*

SCENE: MORIARTY'S *yacht.*

HOLMES *and* WATSON *are seated together, bound to their chairs. The time bomb continues to tick. On deck the* THREE KILLERS *are standing guard. Music of military bands can be heard in the distance.*

WATSON

There's the Royal Malta Artillery Corps.

HOLMES

It's the Singapore Police.

WATSON

I think you're mistaken.

HOLMES

I know I'm not.

WATSON

It's the Royal—

HOLMES

Singapore Police!

(*The distant music changes.*)

WATSON

You would not deny *that* to be the Ceylon Militia.

(*The distant music changes again.*)

HOLMES

Followed by the Dyaks of Borneo.

WATSON

Fine chaps.

HOLMES

Good spearsmen.

WATSON

Excellent headhunters.

HOLMES

Gifts for the tribal women.

(*The distant music changes once more.*)

WATSON

Holmes—Holmes, listen! Have you ever heard anything quite as thrilling?

HOLMES

No, my friend. There is nothing to match the 5th Northumberland Fusiliers.

(*Military music fades out.*)

WATSON

The war—our adventures—my dear departed Mary—they seem so clear.

HOLMES

To me as well.

WATSON

I had seen more beautiful women, but never a face that was sweeter or more sensitive in nature.

HOLMES

It was the tale of her father's strange disappearance that intrigued me.

WATSON

That night, as the trail led to Pondicherry Lodge, her hand reached out instinctively for mine—and mine for hers. We rode in the darkness together, like children, and knew that we had nothing to fear. Not then—nor for a lifetime.

A married man,
A married man,
I think of when I was a married man,
For then I found life's purpose and its plan,
Since time began.

A lonely man,
I took a wife,
And added love and laughter to my life,
And I knew then there's no one richer than
A married man.

The joys, the woes, the happiness,
We shared it all, we two.
And oh, the woes seemed so much less,
And how the pleasures grew!

The bachelor,
The bachelor—
I've lived his life, and I have lived with her—
Well, let him lead his so-called merry life as best he can,
But as for me,

I'd rather be
A happy man,
Contented man,
A married man.

HOLMES

I am glad that you have these memories, Watson. I am equally glad that I do not.

WATSON

If I could live my life again,
I'd follow that same plan.
Ah yes, because,
With her I was
A happy man,
Contented man,
A married man.

(Music ends. The ticking of the time bomb fills the cabin.)

How much time is there left?

HOLMES

Tension of mainspring reduced point zero nine. Two minutes to detonation.

(The THREE GANG MEMBERS *enter. The* FIRST GANG MEMBER *goes to the deck, and signals the* KILLERS *to leave, then exits himself. The* SECOND GANG MEMBER *goes to the deck, and is about to leave when an* IRREGULAR *pops over the side of the ship, blocking his way.)*

MACIPPER

Got a lump o' coal for a mudlark, mate?

SECOND GANG MEMBER

Get out of my way!

MACIPPER

Open your heart to a poor little lad. I'm the sole support of me mother and dad.

SECOND GANG MEMBER

Now look! You'd better—

(*A* SECOND IRREGULAR *pops over the side of the ship, just behind the* SECOND GANG MEMBER *who is now surrounded.*)

DUCKBELLOWS

Got a lump o' coal for a mudlark, mate?

SECOND GANG MEMBER

Get off this ship! Hurry up!

DUCKBELLOWS

At your service, mate!

(*The two* IRREGULARS *toss the* SECOND GANG MEMBER *over the side. The* THIRD GANG MEMBER, *who has been testing* HOLMES'S *and* WATSON'S *ropes, now goes to the deck.* WIGGINS *appears in front of him.*)

WIGGINS

That's a right nice coat you got, mate. Brass buttons and no mistake.

THIRD GANG MEMBER

Let go of my coat!—

WIGGINS

I'll swap yer a Dunlop tyre for it!

THIRD GANG MEMBER

—I said let go!

(IRENE *enters up the gangplank. With her purse she hits the* THIRD GANG MEMBER *over the head, knocking him to the deck where he lies stunned.*)

WIGGINS

Good work, Miss Adler!

IRENE

It was nothing, boys. (*Takes a brick out of her purse, and shows it to them.*)

THIRD GANG MEMBER

Get me off this ship! Or we'll all be killed! Get me off! ! !

(*The* IRREGULARS *oblige the* GANG MEMBER *by tossing him over the side. They exit down the gangplank.* IRENE *descends to the cabin.*)

WATSON

Miss Adler!

IRENE

A bomb!

WATSON

Yes.

(IRENE *moves toward it*)

HOLMES

Don't touch it!

IRENE

Isn't there something I can —

HOLMES

No! (*rising and dropping off his bonds*) You see, it is an extremely delicate instrument, and must be neutralized by an expert only.

WATSON

Holmes! What on earth —

HOLMES

Some day I must teach you the Malay grip. When your hands are clasped in that manner, it is quite impossible to bind them securely.

WATSON

You might have said something to me—

HOLMES

I did not for an excellent reason. The guns of our guards were quite real. And of all your splendid traits, my dear Watson, the concealment of emotion is not one. Be very still, Miss Adler. (IRENE *freezes.* HOLMES *looks around the room, then quickly removes a picture of Queen Victoria, and rips off its wire. He lowers the wire into the ticking mechanism of the bomb—slowly, cautiously. There is an almost unbearable wait. Then in one quick movement* HOLMES *twists his hand a quarter turn, and suddenly the machine stops.*) Von Herder seldom varies the position of his mainspring. (*crosses to* WATSON *and unties him*) Now my dear Watson, if you will be so good as to find me a carriage, I shall lose no time in pursuing the gems.

WATSON

Of course. (*starts for the deck, then turns back to* IRENE) Thank you very much for coming, Miss Adler. (*exits*)

HOLMES

It was a completely irrational act. You put your life in needless danger.

IRENE

I thought yours was.

HOLMES

I will admit that in finding me here you have shown a degree of astuteness and courage not commonly found in a woman. This — cannot help but stir up within me — a feeling of —

IRENE

Yes . . . ?

HOLMES

— gratitude.

IRENE

Thanks.

HOLMES

I shall have Dr. Watson keep you informed of all further developments in this case.

IRENE

That's very kind of you.

(WATSON *enters on deck.*)

WATSON

(*calling down the steps*)

Holmes! Bit of luck. I found a four-wheeler at the end of the pier. He's waiting.

HOLMES

Good bye, Miss Adler, and thank you very much. (*calling to deck*) Watson! I'll drop you off at Baker Street. (HOLMES *and* WATSON *exit.*)

IRENE

It was my pleasure, Mr. Holmes,
Just my pleasure —
Rushing here to save you on the run.

ACT II

SCENE 3

TIME: *That night.*

SCENE: *The cutaway of a horse-drawn carriage bouncing and joggling along at top speed. (Music underscores.)*

HOLMES, *seated in the carriage, stares straight ahead in silence. There is a look of faint perplexity on his face.*

HOLMES

(calls to coachman)

Keep to the Canterbury Road!

(to himself, spoken in time to music)

—Now his balloon will not go more than six hours
Without refueling, and so his only chance
Is to board it somewhere on the south coast
And fly across the Channel into France.
But where?——

(Over the music of the racing carriage the music of IRENE'S *song surges up, as he is distracted from his deductions by thoughts of her. He struggles to concentrate.* IRENE'S *music dies away.)*

—The problem is where—oh yes—of course—
He'll choose the nearest coastal town to London,
For he's got to leave the country by tonight,
And the nearest coastal town is—Folkestone—
Folkestone! Folkestone! That's right!!—
——No, I'm
Wrong!——No—
—He'd never go to Folkestone—

It's June, and it's a honeymoon resort.
Those spooning couples are about! Oh no,
He'll choose some more secluded Channel port.
But which?—It's obviously—

(*Once again* IRENE's *music wells up as he is distracted by thoughts of her, and dies away as he drives her out of his mind.*)

——Yes——
Another port——Hythe!
Those skulls at St. Leonards by the Sea!
He'd relish a touch of the macabre—
Hythe! Yes, that's where he'll be!

Hythe?——It can't possibly
Be Hythe! What's the matter with my brain?!

Hythe is at sea level——
——He'll need a high terrain—
Yes, a higher elevation——
For the ratio of air to gas volume
Compares with the ballast ratio—
—He'll need at least four hundred feet—

—And now I know where we will meet!
——The search is over!—
The cliffs of Dover!
(*calls to coachman*)
On to Dover!
Yes, Dover!

Blackout

ACT II

SCENE 4

TIME: *Later that night.*

SCENE: *A precipice on the cliffs of Dover. We discover* PROFESSOR MORIARTY *standing at the edge, waving a lantern skyward in a measured pattern. There is a satchel beside him.*

After several moments HOLMES *appears on the cliff behind* MORIARTY. *For a while there is no sound but the whistling of the wind.*

HOLMES

Good evening, Professor. (MORIARTY *quickly puts out the lantern.*) You need not have put out the lantern, as you remain quite visible against the stars. Your head now eclipses Corona Borealis.

MORIARTY

My dismay is also eclipsed — but only by my admiration, Holmes. I did not imagine that even you could triumph over a perfect machine.

HOLMES

The machine had one defect. It was made by a man.

MORIARTY

An acknowledgment of human weakness? That does not sound like you.

HOLMES

You shall know it is me soon enough, Professor.

MORIARTY

I suppose you intend to kill me.

HOLMES

Hypothesis correct!

MORIARTY

It would accomplish nothing, Holmes. For the evil that men do lives after them.

HOLMES

(*pointing to* MORIARTY'S *satchel*)

And is frequently carried about in their luggage.

MORIARTY

Did you think I'd be foolish enough to have the gems in my possession? (*tosses the satchel to* HOLMES) You *are* out of sorts tonight, Holmes.

HOLMES

Then you've left them in London.

MORIARTY

Surely I should be asking the questions, as I now have a pistol aimed at your heart.

HOLMES

A pistol you dare not use within earshot of Dover Castle and its garrison of troops.

MORIARTY

Hypothesis false! The wind is south by southeast, and would deflect the sound of the shot. What is wrong with you, Holmes? Your logic tonight seems strangely impaired. Can it be that you have allowed a corrosive factor to enter your delicately balanced mind?

HOLMES

What rot!

MORIARTY

Can it be that we are no longer equals? That I, in fact, have gained the advantage?

HOLMES

Absurd!

MORIARTY

But if my hypothesis is correct, the absurdity is yours—and the victory mine.

HOLMES

(*lunging at* MORIARTY)

Hypothesis false!

(*They struggle on the edge of the cliff for several moments, then both fall off the precipice. Music underscores with violence and terrible finality. There is a diminishing scream as*)

Lights fade out

ACT II

SCENE 5

TIME: *A few days later.*

SCENE: *An area representing a part of* London.

To the sonorous tolling of funeral bells, two funeral processions, going in opposite directions, pass each other solemnly. Each has its own coffin. One is made up of MORIARTY'S *friends; the other, of those who were loyal to* SHERLOCK HOLMES. *The processions pass from view, as*

Lights come up slowly on . . .

ACT II

SCENE 6

TIME: *Later that day.*

SCENE: *The Baker Street flat.*

We discover DR. WATSON *writing his memoirs. There is a knocking at the door.*

WATSON

Come in.

(MRS. HUDSON *enters, holding a newspaper article.*)

MRS. HUDSON

Has the Doctor seen the paper?

WATSON

Not yet, Mrs. Hudson.

MRS. HUDSON

(*showing article*)

He's been given the Order of Merit—post-humorously. Had he lived, he'd have been bestowed with knighthood.

WATSON

Honors meant little to him.

MRS. HUDSON

I suppose the Doctor will want me to clean up the papers, and put all the chemical acids away—and I'll have a man come in to fill up the bullet holes in the wall—one of these days.

(Dabs her eyes, then pulls herself together and goes to the door. As she exits, crosses paths with IRENE, *who enters.)*

WATSON

Miss Adler! — I'm terribly sorry.

IRENE

I've come to say good bye, Dr. Watson.

WATSON

You're going back to America?

IRENE

Tonight. On the midnight steamer.

WATSON

But you will come to England again?

IRENE

(*a pause as she looks around the room*)

His things — his books — what will become of them now?

WATSON

He's left them to the Boys Ragged School in George Yard.

IRENE

I'm glad he did that. (*glancing at papers on desk*) Your memoirs?

WATSON

Our last adventures together. You look — very lovely today.

IRENE

I never mourn for good memories, Doctor.

WATSON

I'll make some tea—

(He scoops up a pile of manuscripts from the desk, and takes them to a nearby shelf. We are immediately aware of a smoldering pipe, the only remaining object on the desk.)

IRENE

I'm afraid I don't have time, Dr. Watson. I still have most of my packing to do.

WATSON

I quite—(*stops abruptly, noticing the smoldering pipe*)—I quite understand. (*He walks casually back to the desk, picks up the pipe, and begins to puff on it.*) You'll write to me of course, Miss Adler.

IRENE

Did you think you had to ask? We shall always be friends, Dr. Watson. We shall always have him in common.

(She kisses him on the cheek, and exits. WATSON *sits down. A moment later* HOLMES *enters from the adjoining room.)*

HOLMES

Very clever of you, my dear Watson. You have unexplored possibilities. Now—to continue . . . as we fell from the top, I grasped a stout vine that grew vertically down the face of the cliff. While holding on for my life, I heard Moriarty's horrible scream ending abruptly several hundred feet below. It was then that I hit upon a most satisfactory plan. I would toss my coat and waistcoat over the side of the cliff to give evidence of my death, and remain out of sight for three days until—(*a pause*) You're not writing.

WATSON

I don't like this at all, Holmes.

HOLMES

You find the plan fallible?

WATSON

Infallible and inhuman.

HOLMES

My dear fellow—

WATSON

Why must you be living this lie? Moriarty is dead. Captain Gregg is under arrest—

HOLMES

And the Jubilee gems are still missing, not to mention Moriarty's lieutenants—five dangerous men determined to continue the professor's work. Believing me dead, they will now become careless, thus making my job much simpler.

WATSON

That, of course, is the only reason.

HOLMES

What the devil are you talking about?

WATSON

I think you know what I'm talking about, and *whom* I'm talking about.

HOLMES

What rubbish!

WATSON

Does she terrify you so much that you have to hide in a coffin?

HOLMES

The scheme has nothing to do with her! It is only to recover the gems! — (WATSON *exits to his bedroom*) — *the gems!*

(*Two distinct knocks are heard at the front door.* HOLMES *crosses to it swiftly, and knocks once in response. Three knocks are returned.* HOLMES *opens the door to admit* WIGGINS *and some of the* IRREGULARS.)

WIGGINS

We've got the lot. Everything on that ship you wanted, sir.

HOLMES

Excellent, Wiggins. On the laboratory table! (*The* IRREGULARS *run downstage, and deposit near the laboratory table a multitude of personal objects that belonged to* PROFESSOR MORIARTY. *The* IRREGULARS *scamper out of the flat, as* HOLMES *and* WIGGINS *come downstage.* HOLMES *starts scraping dust from the various objects into an array of test tubes.*) Somewhere . . . somewhere among Moriarty's possessions lies a clue to the whereabouts of the gems. Of that I am certain.

WIGGINS

Likewise, sir.

HOLMES

He would of course have inspected the intended hiding place prior to the crime.

WIGGINS

Correct.

HOLMES

And when he did, an element in the location would by all natural laws have adhered to something he wore or carried.

WIGGINS

My very thought.

HOLMES

It is left for us to detect the element, and to fix it geographically.

WIGGINS

Which we are well equipped to do.

HOLMES

Quite. (*turning on various pieces of laboratory equipment*) Heat . . . Catalyst . . . Reagent . . . Coils for induction . . . Mark! (*lights dim in rest of room*) First, I will add a bit of hydrochloric acid to the solution—a blue precipitate will indicate the presence of lead, and thus narrow the field to Shropshire, North Wales, or the Isle of Man—(*a pause*)—test negative . . . Well, no matter. By boiling the solution, and adding ammonia, I will know at once whether iron is present. The purity of ore will tell me very quickly whether Cumberland or North Lancashire is the place to visit—(*a pause*)—test negative . . . What next? What next? Some phosphoric acid salts may point to the caustic soda beds of Prussia—but do not—It must be here somewhere! It must be! Ah, yes. This tiny fragment embedded in the bottom of his boot—so small it nearly eluded me—(*with wooden tweezers he passes the fragment through the electric spark*)—When volatized by a spark from the induction coil, it may well show the spectral characteristics of a substance that is known as . . . (*forlornly*) the substance of a heel. What else, what else? It must be here somewhere. I'm sure of it. (*Then for the first time he notices something previously untouched. A light comes into his eyes. Music underscores as he picks up a book from* MORIARTY'S *possessions. Music stops as* HOLMES *begins to read from the book.*) Friends, Romans, countrymen, lend me your ears—I come to bury . . .

(*Lights fade on* HOLMES *and* WIGGINS, *as lights come up full on* BAXTER *and* CRIMINALS *assembled for funeral service*)

ACT II

SCENE 7

TIME: *That night.*

SCENE: *A private funeral chapel where* BAXTER *is addressing the* CRIMINAL MOURNERS. *A boy sits at an organ playing solemn music softly.*

BAXTER

. . . bury our dear, departed friend, Professor James Moriarty. Your shining countenances would have warmed the professor's heart. A heart as big as all the world, his legacy to us.

I shall miss you, James
I shall . . .

(*A* MAN *and* TWO WOMEN *enter.*)

Alderman Purdy and constituents.

I shall miss you, James.

(*An* ELDERLY WOMAN *enters.*)

Nurse Molly Craven — friend to young women.

(*An extremely* TALL WOMAN, *wearing a black veil, is seen at the door.*)

Ahh, Mrs. Heggars. Come in, come in. To those of you who do not know Mrs. Heggars, may I say that she is Liverpool's foremost opium dealer.

(*A* WOMAN *enters, followed by* TWO TARTS.)

Mrs. Wakefield and her nieces.

CRIMINALS

Rest in peace, dear James,
Rest in peace.

(*An* ELDERLY MAN *dressed as a deacon enters.*)

BAXTER

Our defrocked deacon of Dover.

CRIMINALS

We lament, dear James,
Your decease.
We shall mourn as we have never mourned before
For Professor Moriarty is no more.

(A FRAIL-LOOKING OLD MAN *with a beard and heavy lensed glasses enters.*)

BAXTER

Von Herder of Berlin. His torture devices were things of pure joy to the professor.

'Tis appropriate that we
Should behold him once again.
Raise the lid that we may see
This most generous of men.

CRIMINALS

Oh hail!
Farewell!
We shall miss . . .

(BAXTER *signals to the* THREE KILLERS *to raise the lid of the coffin. Revealed is no corpse, but a huge mound of glittering gems. The* CRIMINALS *gasp, and freeze in astonishment.*)

BAXTER

We'll dispense with the reading of the will.

Ooh!
What jewel–ler–y!

CRIMINALS

(*scooping up the gems*)

Lots and lots of jewellery!
Hang it on me

And no Christmas tree
Is half so grand!

BAXTER

Give me glittery things—

CRIMINALS

Emeralds and pearly strings,
Ruby rings
On every finger
Of my hand!

MAN

I'll wear them all the time,
Not only for Sunday best.

WOMAN

Unless I've got me baubles on,

CRIMINALS

Me pretty little baubles on
I feel undressed!
Out on Leicester Square
Diamonds down to my derriere!
Everyone there—
'll stop and stare.
They'll all kowtow!
Don't show me cash—
It's merely paper trash!
Enough o' that tomfoolery!
Butter me up with jewellery!
Clutter me up with jewellery now!

Stock my jewellery box
Chockablock with luverly rocks!
Stuff me pockets 'n' stuff me socks
And underwear!

Look at 'em flashing!
Isn't it smashing!
Look at 'em,
Look at 'em,
Isn't it dashing!
Give me jewellery, dear.
Deck me out from 'ere to 'ere.
Say that I look like a chandelier
But I don't care!
Look at them bangles!
Look at them spangles!
Look at the way that they dingles 'n' dangles!

Some folks need alcohol to get in the proper mood
But all I need's my trinkets on
My inky-dinky trinkets on
And I'm half-stewed!

See me out on the street
Drippin' jewels from 'ead to feet—
Even the millionaires I meet'll scrape and bow!
Don't need no clothes—
Just rows and rows
Of nice shiny jewellery!
Cover me up with jewellery!
Smuvver me up with jewellery now.

Out on Leicester Square—
Diamonds down to my derriere!
Everyone there—
'll stop and stare.
They'll all kowtow!
Set me ablaze!
Set me alight!
Brighter than Parliament
On Guy Fawkes Night!

Polish me off,
Demolish me off with jewellery
Right now!

BAXTER

Anyone not satisfied with his share?

(*Throwing off his* VON HERDER *disguise,* HOLMES *faces* BAXTER.)

HOLMES

Just one, my friend — Her Majesty, the Queen!

(HOLMES *blows a whistle. Almost at once* WIGGINS *appears in the doorway with* POLICEMEN. *The* POLICEMEN *rush in and seize the* CRIMINALS.)

WIGGINS

Right on time, eh Mr. Holmes?

HOLMES

Excellent, Wiggins. I couldn't have done it without you.

WIGGINS

I quite agree, sir.

(WIGGINS *exits. A moment later* INSPECTOR LESTRADE *runs in.*)

LESTRADE

Holmes! Well, I'll be damned! I knew in my heart you couldn't be dead!

HOLMES

I am deeply touched, Inspector. And thank you for the memorial wreath.

LESTRADE

The very least we could do. How the devil did you know where to find the gems?

HOLMES

Moriarty himself could not resist telling me just a few minutes before he died. I merely completed the quotation he gave me.

LESTRADE

Quotation?

HOLMES

The evil that men do lives after them — (*turning to the coffin*) the good is oft interred with their bones.

LESTRADE

Ah, deduction! I shall have to try that someday. (*to* POLICEMEN) Thompson — Whittaker — (*the* TWO POLICEMEN *pick up the coffin*) Easy now. Easy. Don't let her tip.

(LESTRADE *and* POLICEMEN *exit with the coffin, leaving only* HOLMES *and the* BOY ORGANIST *on stage.* HOLMES *sits down and lights his pipe, all but ignoring the* BOY, *who continues playing the organ softly.*)

HOLMES

You may remove your disguise. I know who you are.

(*The* BOY *removes a cap, and shakes out an abundance of hair. It is* IRENE.)

IRENE

I didn't expect to fool you.

HOLMES

I presume you observed my pipe on the doctor's desk, and followed me here from the flat.

IRENE

Precisely.

HOLMES

To what purpose, Miss Adler?

IRENE

I was rather involved with your case. I just wanted to see how it would end.

HOLMES

Ah yes. And now—

IRENE

And now I go home. I'm sailing tonight on the midnight steamer.

HOLMES

You are a remarkable woman, Miss Adler.

IRENE

That cannot help but stir up within me a feeling of . . .

HOLMES

Yes—

IRENE

Gratitude. (*a pause*) Mr. Holmes, you are a fool!

HOLMES

Madam?

IRENE

For all your brilliant deductions, a fool. I could have given you an adventure beyond your wildest dreams. In feelings you have never known before. Feelings that are not grit, but stimulation to the sensitive, reasoning mind. What a pity that Sherlock Holmes has chosen to leave a mystery unsolved. (*exits*)

(*Music underscores as* HOLMES *considers what she has said.*)

HOLMES

It's all so simple
So very simple—

(WATSON *enters from stage right, carrying* HOLMES'S *cloak and deerstalker cap.*)

WATSON

I heard you got them!

HOLMES

(*dejectedly*)

They fell into my trap—like Bengal tigers into a shikari's pit.

WATSON

I have a carriage waiting.

(*As* HOLMES *puts on his cloak and cap,* MORIARTY'S VOICE *is heard.*)

MORIARTY'S VOICE

O Julius Caesar! Thou art mighty yet! Thy spirit walks abroad. But freedom can be dreary, Holmes. Dreary without the spice and sting of an equal battle, battle, battle, battle, . . .

(HOLMES *and* WATSON *search frantically for the source of* MORIARTY'S VOICE, *which continues as on a broken record. Finally* HOLMES *releases a panel under the keyboard of the organ, and pulls out a recording cylinder.* MORIARTY'S VOICE *stops suddenly.*)

HOLMES

Of course he would be alive! If one vine, why not two!

WATSON

But he fell from the cliff! You saw him!

HOLMES

I heard a scream diminishing into the distance! Of course—a simple ventriloquist's trick! (*Lights pull in around* HOLMES *and* WATSON, *as they move downstage.*) And worse, he foresaw all that has happened since. By giving me a clue to the whereabouts of the gems, he has managed to keep me quite busy while he has ample time to escape from England. (*As the lights come up,* HOLMES *and* WATSON *are revealed, standing in front of* 221B *Baker Street.*) I shall find him if I have to search the four corners of the earth.

WATSON

But where will you start?

HOLMES

With luck I can catch the eight-thirty train to Southampton, and there board the midnight steamer to Charleston. (*They shake hands.*) Good bye, old friend.

(HOLMES *starts to leave.*)

WATSON

Holmes—(HOLMES *pauses.*)—that's in America.

HOLMES

Precisely.

(HOLMES *turns upstage and disappears into the fog.* WATSON *begins to smile and wonder as the*)

Curtain falls